Home Life

Home Life

poems

JON BISHOP

OPEN ROAD
INTEGRATED MEDIA
NEW YORK

All rights reserved, including without limitation the right to reproduce this book or any portion thereof in any form or by any means, whether electronic or mechanical, now known or hereinafter invented, without the express written permission of the publisher.

These are works of fiction. Names, characters, places, events, and incidents either are the product of the author's imagination or are used fictitiously. Any resemblance to actual persons, living or dead, businesses, companies, events, or locales is entirely coincidental.

Copyright © 2024 by Jon Bishop

ISBN: 978-1-5040-9807-6

This edition published in 2025 by God of the Desert Books/Open Road Integrated Media, Inc.
180 Maiden Lane
New York, NY 10038
www.openroadmedia.com

To my family

Home Life

REALITY

The body begins life
perfect, unblemished,
not different than the soul that inhabits it—
pure but without language.

But then the cracks come.
Some slippage.
The wall, clear and thick and strong,
is now spidered with

fractures, as if it has drawn a map
of its eventual crumbling.

And isn't this how it always is?
How things new and bright
will slowly break—
with wisdom comes creaking knees—
until, eventually, it all becomes dust
and blows away in the late evening wind.

BOMBOGENESIS

Bombogenesis sounds like some kind of drug you do on the weekends, those big parties on the weekends, the ones where everyone is writhing, writhing, dancing and writhing to music that bangs and shrieks, stuff you'd listen to only while under the influence of "bombogenesis."

Or it's something you say when a really great thing happens to you, something you never expected—like the girl you've always had a crush on said yes when you asked her on a date or you landed your dream job—and so you look up at the sky and pump your fist and yell "bombogenesis."

Or maybe it's when you can't explain the world, either the physical or the metaphysical one, and so you stare out the window and watch swirling clouds blast snow to the ground and you see that snow carried about by the wind and, awed and humbled, you whisper: "bombogenesis."

ROAD RAGE

Cars frozen
like a river in winter.
And your anger builds,
volcanic,
shifting the sky from blue to blood,
fires everywhere,
explosions on the highway
like lights switching on in late evening,

but then,
a breath,
a balm cascading into your lungs
and zigging
through your zagged veins,
and you smile,
because life itself,
forever careening forward,

has hit pause,
an eremitic break
from the chaos
of this unrelenting world.

CAREERS

Last night, the mountains cracked,
gray stone smashed to earth,
pluming the dust into the sky,

then I woke up, gasped,
choked on dust not there,
and put on my uniform,

the one dusty itself,
ripped and not yet fixed,
and I remember I was once

joy-filled, fun, a fixture
at the office for twenty years,
a friend, a colleague, a guide,

but then gone, unceremoniously,
career vanished, life vanished,
a year of pain, years of pain;

now nothing but maintenance work—
fine, but not the dream,
shattered like the rocks,

sizzled and gone like an aging star,
and you, smiling, telling me I'm so nice,
so needed, so good at what I do.

ROOTLESSNESS

I tried to go home once.
I tried to listen to what you said—

that this is what we're supposed to do;
we're supposed to come,

like the animals yearly,
back to this soft and safe place.

But I saw houses staring
with vacant and empty eyes,

ready to lunge forward, bare fangs,
and sink siding into your neck

and drain your blood,
so they can deepen their outer red.

You're tossed to the side, then, crisp and dried,
a piece of prey done with, ready to blow away,

like celestial dust shaved from an interstellar collision,
sullen and lonely as it traverses the black of the universe.

So I couldn't get beyond the entranceway. Sorry.
I knew what was waiting. And why.

CHAIR

It's like this:
You'll shout and protest,
but as you do,
I'll turn my chair to the wall
and stare at the brown—
the floors, the siding,
each cracked with age,
like my skin, litanies
of lines and stress,

knifed into permanence
with your excuses, your violence,
like subjecting me to this
spittle-soaked rant,
here in the dim-dark.
And do you see me now?
This chair, the one you gave me,
is smashed in the back,
is sinking but still standing,
is. Just is. Like me. And I'll keep it
flipped and away,
a makeshift monument,
so I don't have to hear
the plume of your bootsteps
on the dirt and the
grumbling motor giving way
to silence, then oblivion.
But the oblivion is for you, not me.
Because I'm the one who will stay.

RECURRENCE

Loneliness always recurs
in the dark of night,
in the darkness of this house,
this empty, creaking house.

The pangs fade
in the day,
in the distractions
of the day,

burying themselves
below surface,
like ticks under skin,
then emerge

when I come home.
No one to greet me.
All meals alone.
And no calls on the phone.

This is the saddest
I have been.
Is this punishment
for my sins?

EVENTURUM

The terror of singed love
burning in the dark of night,
where you, alone,
sniff the salted air
and weep,
like your mother did
in late February
twenty years ago,
when your father,

drunk,
stumbled in,
like a dizzied and bleeding bull
struck with an arrow
or maybe a bullet,
but we're getting into semantics now,
because she asked
where were you?
and he, burning,
balled his hand
and smashed her face
and she fell over,
clutching herself,
and pierced the sky
with her cries,
like a baby,
breaking the silence
of a midnight home,
and you stood there,
scared,
motionless,
watching all this happen,

because you were six
and what were you supposed to do,
other than stare?
Like now,
you're silent
watching the lapping waves,
(this sea of tears)
wondering why he said those things last night,
wondering why he hit you.
But you know why.
Because it's a cycle,
like the motion of the salted air,
like the tides.

WORK

Winter comes and, like a good teacher,
shows us the real meaning of work—

the few daylight hours spent
with people we like

or people we barely know,
a break

before the sky empties and
our bones crackle, first

with loneliness, then
with the cold.

HANGOVER

See the red morning billowing
like the fire-breath of a volcano
roaring in the trembling predawn dark
and spewing heat across the mountains,
but there are buildings here, instead of mountains,
and you ache like you've been scorched
from the innards of the earth,
each breath like a tree blazed and creaking

and then crumbling to dirt.
But you can't stay here forever, stuck
to sweat-soaked plush, and so you choke yourself
up,
stand, and your eyes, red like the sky,
glance up and down, and you can't help but stare
at this great glorious thing, this red river,
like the blood sinewing through your veins,
giving way, slowly, to blue, then, finally,
to calming, reassuring light.

RESIGNATIONS

Gray skies always
and night eternal
(reality dull and unrelenting)
in this moment, mind blank,

your face the same,
where there were once
moments of feeling,
of head high, shoulders back,

breaths deep and full,
full of air crisp and clean,
fuel for late-night drinks
and football on empty fields

at night, illuminated by soft light,
and racing across sidewalks
like cats with eyes for fleeing mice,
a hunger,

a desire, general and driving,
and for her, the queen, the one
everyone wanted—and she was
yours, briefly, then, like everything then,

it ended, fleeting, like a blink,
like the flush of your face
after you kissed
or when you tripped

and skinned your knee
on a pockmarked street.
A new start, fresh, but no,
just a face in the crowd,

a phantom, or perhaps even less—
a molecule in a wave,
lolling slowly to shore,
one unit, nothing else visible—

and lesser, and lesser still,
until the shoulders slump
and the voice becomes weak
and the head stays bent,

eyes on the blacktop,
the perpetual shadow of the street,
and there is no point
in lifting your head,

your vision cateracted with bleakness,
the typing for eight hours a day,
the phone calls, the cheery messages
left online, exhorting everyone and all

to buy things unneeded, to call and order,
(unrelenting, unrelenting)

where they won't talk to you, because
your voice is too soft and meek,

your body like a pumpkin left outside
for months—shriveled and moldy and
imploded, a thing once proud and visible,
something once seen,

your dead self weighted and dangling,
but like the pumpkin, no possibility
for a fruiting next season, so you now,
in the driveway, a thin orange sky

on the way to darkening,
shut your eyes, and you see the things
you once did, who you once were,
and you take solace in this, and breathe.

MORNING GLORIES

In the silence of the morning,
sky black like coal unburned,
I'm watching—

wind cold, face colder—
in one of the trees, thin
and nearly leafless,

a bird look up
and unburden itself,
crying to the moon,

as if asking it
to stay longer,
as if it knows that,

in thirty minutes or so,
the dark will bleed
orange and red and purple,

before fading into
perpetual blue,
almost unnoticed,

unlike the chilled nights
and crisp mornings, with
all those spangled stars.

AN APOCALYPSE

We're like a swirling vortex in the night.
A crash of plates. A shout in dusted air.
This rage will vein throughout the house tonight.

A silent meal and then a booming fight.
A question: did you ever really care?
We're like a swirling vortex in the night.

I wish the public saw us impolite.
(Too soft a word for when you threw a chair.)
This rage will vein throughout the house
tonight.

I've packed my bags. I'm ready for my flight.
I booked it 'cause we're so beyond repair.
We're like a swirling vortex in the night.

You slump into your chair, then shut the light.
You mutter that our love was never there.
This rage will vein throughout the house
tonight.

Our lovely vows were never truly right,
'cause yours were fake, just like an empty prayer.
We're like a swirling vortex in the night.
This rage will vein throughout the house
tonight.

LAST THINGS

Last afternoon, while seated on my porch,
I saw the sun shake loose from the sky.

We all did. This felt like an apocalypse, because
it was, and so there we all were, barely visible,

looking up at the pockmarks of stars on the
black,
the forever and the long ago visible now,

and we didn't care that the great gaseous star
that spews fire and light

had disappeared somewhere into the universe,
because the temperature was falling

like snow at midnight in December,
one degree, two degrees, three,

each flake another drop,
and we drew closer together

and threw our arms around one another,
flesh joining flesh, mind joining mind,

and watched the eons spin like vanes in wind
before all things once again became bright.

ABOUT THE AUTHOR

Jon Bishop began writing at a young age and hasn't stopped since. He began publishing his work in high school and college and then, following graduation, worked as a journalist for four years, honing his abilities. Bishop received his master's degree in English literature, which is when he began to take poetry seriously. After leaving the newspaper business, he decided to focus exclusively on his work as a poet. *Home Life* is his second poetry collection. Bishop lives with his family in New Hampshire.

ABOUT THE PUBLISHER

God of the Desert Books was founded in 2022 by David Swindle and Sally Shideler. The company seeks to bring together creatives across cultural, religious, ideological, and international boundaries to collaborate on books and other artistic endeavors. GOTD publishes a wide variety of titles including nonfiction, genre novels, memoirs, literary books, and poetry. GOTD is a Zionist activist publisher advocating in defense of the Jewish people and all free societies threatened by authoritarian regimes.

Home Life: Poems is the company's second title, following the memoir *Israel Odyssey: Finding Peace in the Middle East* by P. David Hornik."

ABOUT THE IMPRINT

God of the Desert Books offers titles across genres and mediums. For the Oasis of the Desert line of books the publisher presents literary titles including novels and poetry. *Home Life: Poems* is the debut title for the imprint. Please subscribe to our newsletter, OasisOfTheDesert.Substack.com, for articles by our authors and other contributors exploring literature and the arts.

ERUPTION

I saw a storm that broke the sky.
It bled like cattle left for dead.

And then the blood became the flames
That burned throughout the newborn void.

They singed the trees and burned the ground.
They ashed the houses and the cars.

The roads turned black and then caved in.

And gas and heat replaced the air.

The belches cooled. The roaring stopped.
Chaos settled into quiet.

The fires stopped, became the earth.
And life continued on and on.

www.ingramcontent.com/pod-product-compliance
Lightning Source LLC
Chambersburg PA
CBHW021001090426
42736CB00010B/1413